THE VIOLENT EARTH

EARTHQUAKE

JOHN DUDMAN

Thomson Learning
New York

Books in the series

Earthquake
Flood
Storm
Volcano

First published in the
United States in 1993 by
Thomson Learning
115 Fifth Avenue
New York, NY 10003

First published in 1992 by
Wayland (Publishers) Ltd

Library of Congress Cataloging-in-Publication Data

Dudman, John.
    Earthquake / John Dudman.
      p.   c. – (The Violent earth)
    Includes bibliographical references and index.
    Summary: Discusses the causes and effects of earthquakes, examines
the destructive power of historic and modern earthquakes, and
explains how scientists use tools to predict them. Includes related
projects.
    ISBN 1-56847-000-2
    1. Earthquakes–Juvenile literature.   [1. Earthquakes]
I. Title.   II. Series.
QE521.3.D83 1993
551.2'2–dc20
                         92-41510

Printed in Italy

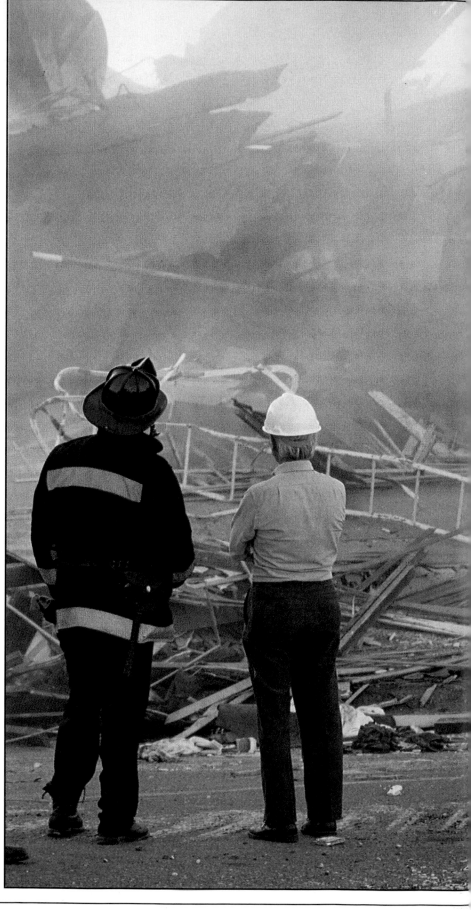

Picture: Relief workers survey the wreckage of old wooden houses in San Francisco after the earthquake struck in 1989.

CONTENTS

A survivor remembers

Marcela Gomez, age ten, was at Sunday school with her five-year-old brother in Chimbote, a port in Peru, when the ground started to tremble violently. Later she remembered, "I grabbed his hand and we ran out into the street. All of a sudden, he left me and ran back inside. He yelled that he had forgotten his bag of candy in the broken building. The noise was terrible. There was a lot of dust, clouds of it everywhere. The dust wrapped around my little brother...I don't remember anything else."

What happened in Peru

Marcela was among the few people who escaped injury in Chimbote on May 31, 1970 when the earthquake struck the Andean mountains overlooking the coast of Peru. More than 300 people died in Chimbote and thousands were hurt. Buildings collapsed as a sudden release of energy underground made the earth roll like ocean

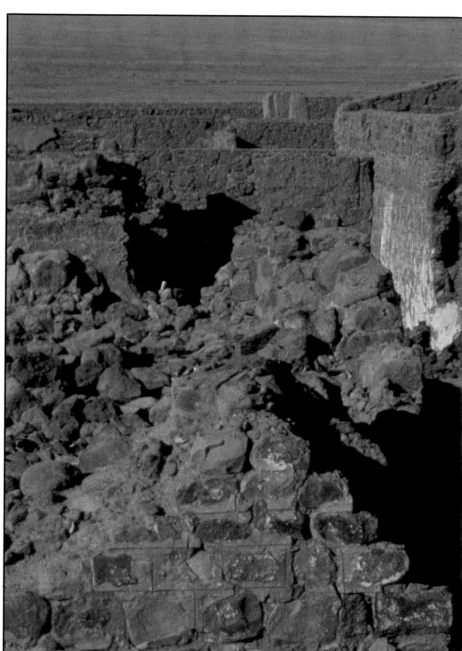

waves. But although the port was shattered it was only a tiny part of the disaster.

The earthquake's violence

The earthquake was so violent that it measured almost 8 on the Richter scale (the scale used to measure earthquakes). Rocks and mudslides fell onto towns and villages as the earthquake tore away a mountainside. A lake spilled over its bank and turned into a waterfall of death.

About 70,000 people were killed and thousands more were injured. More than 800,000 people were made homeless. Big earthquakes like this one are not unusual in some parts of the world. So what causes the earth to shake so violently?

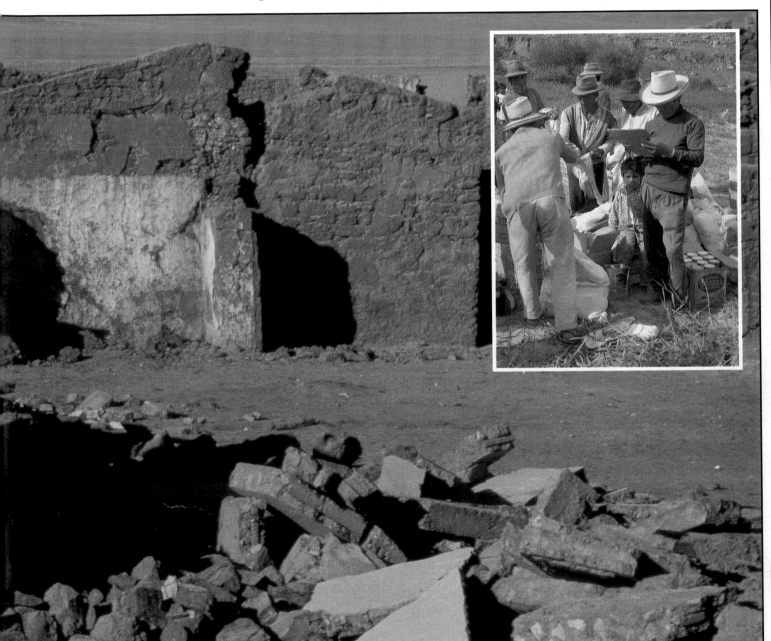

A deserted village in Peru after the 1970 earthquake. (Inset) Earthquake survivors receiving aid.

Inside the earth

The center of the earth is an inferno, which is so hot the surrounding rocks melt. These rocks are part of the enormous plates that lie beneath the outer crust of our planet.

The plates are always moving. Landmasses are made of light material and rest on the moving plates.

For billions of years, big areas of land and ocean have been slowly changing shape as the underground plates slide, grind, and scrape against each other. Today, this activity still goes on. Where the earth's crust is thin, weak, or cracked, such as on some mountain ranges, the heat from inside the earth sometimes comes out in volcanic explosions.

Below: Earthquakes occur mostly at the plate edges where pressure builds up. One plate may be forced to move below the edge of another, causing an earthquake shock.

Crust

Mantle

Above: A section of the earth showing the crust, the mantle, and the fiery core.

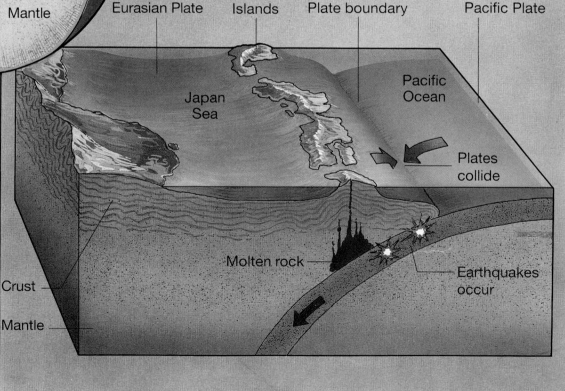

Eurasian Plate   Islands   Plate boundary   Pacific Plate

Japan Sea

Pacific Ocean

Plates collide

Molten rock

Earthquakes occur

Crust

Mantle

Faulting

Earthquakes, too, are caused by the movement of the plates. The plates scrape against each other at the plate boundaries. This builds up pressure that becomes so strong it makes the rocks break along a fracture, or fault. This causes a powerful jolt or earthquake shock. The shock waves travel outward from the focus, which is where most of the movement takes place.

The point on the earth's surface above the focus is called the epicenter. This is where most of the damage caused by the earthquake takes place.

Mechanism of earthquakes

Cutaway

1. Rock is pushed and pulled along fault line.

2. Cracks develop in rock.

3. Rocks break along fault line.

Diagram of an earthquake showing its focus, epicenter, and shock waves.

The dangerous boundaries

More than 300,000 earthquakes whose tremors can be felt occur every year. Others are only slight tremors, which are too light to be noticed. Only a few earthquakes cause major disasters.

In some parts of the world, earthquakes are more likely to happen than in others. The dangerous places for people to live are the areas that lie along the boundaries, or edges of the earth's plates. These areas have very active faults. There is a pattern of more than twenty plate edges that are known to be earthquake zones. Some of these edges follow the coastlines of continents. Others meet beneath oceans and mountain ranges.

Below: The "Ring of Fire" circles the Pacific Ocean from New Zealand up to Japan, crosses eastward, and passes down the coasts of North and South America.

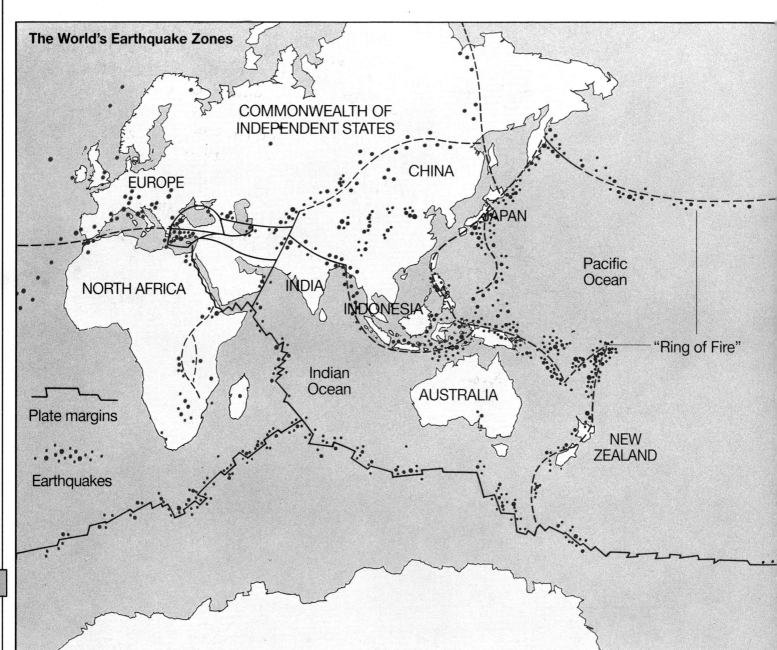

The World's Earthquake Zones

COMMONWEALTH OF INDEPENDENT STATES

CHINA

EUROPE

JAPAN

Pacific Ocean

NORTH AFRICA

INDIA

INDONESIA

"Ring of Fire"

Indian Ocean

AUSTRALIA

Plate margins

Earthquakes

NEW ZEALAND

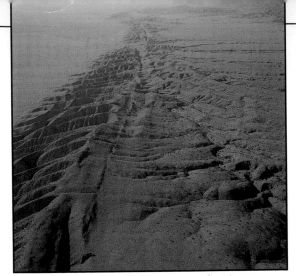

Left: Most plates meet beneath oceans and seas. But the San Andreas fault runs 600 miles along the western coast of California.

"Ring of Fire"

Of all the earthquakes that have been recorded, most have occurred along the edge of the Pacific Plate. This plate follows the coastlines of the Pacific Rim and North and South America. It is known as the "Ring of Fire" because of the volcanoes along its edge.

Other plates share boundaries across the Indian Ocean, through southern China, the Indian Himalayas, and Iran; beneath the deserts of the Middle East, North Africa, and the shores of the Mediterranean; and from the far reaches of the North Atlantic down to south of the Tropic of Capricorn.

NORTH AMERICA

San Andreas Fault

Atlantic Ocean

Mid Atlantic Ridge

SOUTH AMERICA

Twentieth-century Earthquakes
(of over 10,000 deaths)

Date	Place	Deaths (in thousands)
1908	Italy	160
1920	China	180
1923	Japan	143
1935	India	60
1939	Turkey	40
1960	Morocco	12
1970	Peru	70
1972	Nicaragua	12
1976	China	700
1976	Guatemala	23
1988	Armenia	55
1990	Iran	35

Earthquakes in San Francisco

In the Americas, part of the Pacific Plate travels beneath the length of California in a 20-mile-deep crack called the San Andreas Fault. The rocks on either side of the fault are under great strain. Stress is created as the Pacific Plate moves northward about 0.4 inch per year, pushing against the North American Plate, which thrusts southward.

The plate suddenly moves

In 1906 the Pacific Plate suddenly moved 10 feet north. This caused an earthquake in San Francisco that measured 8.25 on the Richter scale. It flattened a huge area of offices, stores, and houses, and fractured gas mains,

The damage to San Francisco at dawn on April 18, 1906 was devastating. After the earthquake destroyed a large part of the city, fire broke out.

"The moment I felt the house tremble... I leaped out of bed and rushed out to the front door...I felt sure the house would fall before I got out. It rocked like a ship on a 'rough sea'. Streams of people...poured into the streets...a mourning, groaning, sobbing, wailing, weeping, and praying crowd. The deathly air [was] very oppressive... quiver after quiver followed...until it seemed as if the very heart of this old earth was broken and was throbbing and dying away slowly and gently." (Eva Atkins Campbell, May 1, 1906.)

A house in San Francisco sagged sideways to the ground during the earthquake that bought widespread damage on October 17, 1989.

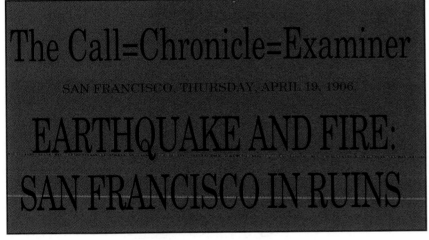

The Call=Chronicle=Examiner

SAN FRANCISCO, THURSDAY, APRIL 19, 1906.

EARTHQUAKE AND FIRE: SAN FRANCISCO IN RUINS

the city had grown bigger over the years.

The earthquake damage

The earthquake everyone expected finally happened at 5:04 p.m. on Tuesday, October 17, 1989, and measured 7.1 on the Richter scale. Luckily scientists were wrong about the huge numbers of casualties. The earthquake killed only 68 people in the city and its outlying areas. Out of the three million people, 3,757 were injured–a low number for such a big city. But 1,400 homes were destroyed and 27,000 businesses damaged. A year after the earthquake, more than one billion dollars had been spent repairing roads, homes, and offices, with much more work still to be carried out in the city.

causing fires to start. About 700 people died, and 250,000 were made homeless in the disaster.

Waiting for disaster

For years afterwards, American scientists studied records; they forecast that another major earthquake would happen in San Francisco. This was likely to be an even greater disaster because

13

Mexico City

On September 19, 1985, Mexico City was rocked by an earthquake that measured 8.1 on the Richter scale. It demolished nearly half the capital in one of the greatest disasters to strike Central America in this century.

The cause of the earthquake

Mexico's ordeal began 217 miles west of the capital. The Cocos Plate, which moves beneath the lighter American Plate, snapped 12 miles below the surface. This produced a massive earthquake, which sent shock waves racing inland.

Rescuers sifting through a heap of concrete after the earthquake hit Mexico City in 1985.

The cutaway diagram shows how two plates collide deep under the ground. Inset maps show the epicenter and position of the Mexico City earthquake.

The earthquake's violence

The first shocks were gentle warnings. Then, with tremendous violence and a roar like an express train hurtling along underground, the big one struck. In a few terrifying minutes, 7,000 people were killed and thousands more injured.

Hotels, schools, offices, cathedrals, churches, and houses were flattened or tossed across streets. Skyscrapers swayed like trees caught in a hurricane, then collapsed, burying hundreds of people beneath them. An apartment building eight stories high sank to a quarter of its size with much of its roof still in place. Some buildings that survived the shock were left leaning at dangerous angles.

"A mighty blow from hell"

"Mexico has been hit with the force of a mighty blow from hell," was how one television reporter described the earthquake, which brought rescue teams from Britain and the United States to explore the mountains of rubble for the thousands of trapped victims. The series of tremors had lasted only a few minutes.

"The building started swaying all over the place before it collapsed. We just held on to each other and prayed." (Scott Thomason, American tourist.)

Earthquakes that occur in any densely populated area like Mexico City usually cause great devastation, as buildings are not earthquake-proof. On July 28, 1976, an earthquake focused on the highly populated industrial city of Tangshan in China.

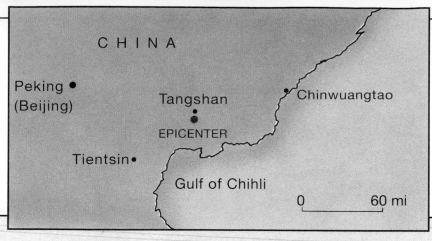

CHINA

Peking (Beijing) •

Tangshan •
EPICENTER

• Chinwuangtao

Tientsin •

Gulf of Chihli

0   60 mi

Shock flattens Chinese city

Before an earthquake occurs, minor tremors are usually felt. But the earthquake in China arrived without warning. Between 650,000 and 750,000 people died as a shock of 8.3 on the Richter scale almost completely destroyed Tangshan. Buildings shook in the capital of Peking (Beijing) 100 miles away. Strong tremors continued for several days. The remaining 100,000 residents fled to makeshift camps in the surrounding countryside. When the last tremor raced through the city, hardly a building was left standing, and all its coal mines had been flooded.

Rebuilding Tangshan

In rebuilding Tangshan, the city was planned so that all the apartment buildings, offices, and factories were designed to resist earthquakes. Parks instead of homes were built on ground above the fault lines. Within two years, people were living and working in the city. By the early 1980s, the number of people in Tangshan was the same as before the earthquake struck.

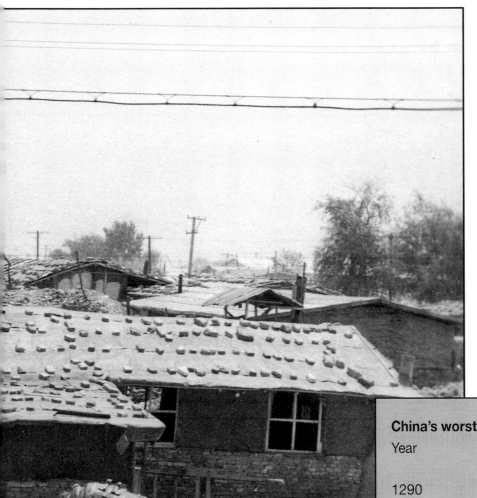

This was one of the first photographs to be taken of Tangshan after the 1976 earthquake.

China's worst earthquakes

Year	Official deaths (in thousands)	Affected area
1290	100	China
1556	830	Shensi province
1668	50	Shantung province
1731	100	Peking (Beijing)
1739	50	China
1920	200	Kansu province
1927	40	Nan Mountains
1932	70	Kansu province
1970	10	S. Yunnan province
1976	700	Tangshan

A rescue team searching for survivors trapped in the rubble at Spitak in 1988.

Armenian disaster

One of the most devastating earthquakes ever recorded on the Richter scale took place in the Republic of Armenia on December 7, 1988. Seismographs recorded a magnitude of nearly 7 as the shock flattened all the buildings taller than eight stories high in the city of Leninakan. Huge cracks appeared in the road to Spitak, a town with a population of 20,000 inhabitants which was described as "utterly destroyed." Officially 55,000 people died in the two towns, but many thousands more are believed to have been killed.

Rescue attempts

After the earthquake struck, survivors wandered stunned through city streets, many gathering around camp fires for warmth. Soldiers set up tent cities for people from devastated regions. They tried to restore electricity and water supplies but lack of equipment prevented officials from launching a major rescue operation.

Officials needed heavy machines like bulldozers that could clear the streets of rubble, but these were not available. This meant that ambulances were not able to reach injured victims. Fortunately, other countries came to their aid by sending in fleets of aircraft carrying relief supplies for the 500,000 people who were left homeless in the freezing temperatures.

Below: Pre-fabricated buildings for earthquake survivors are unloaded from a cargo aircraft.

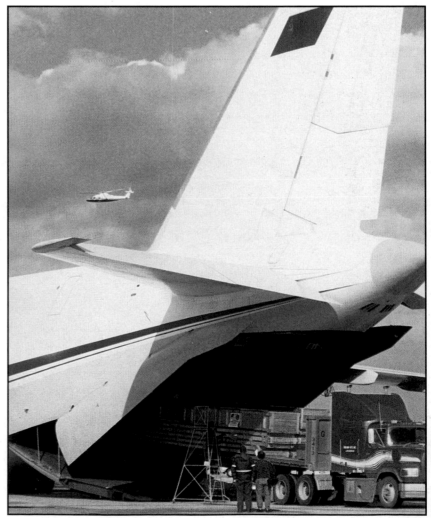

For hundreds of years, scientists have been looking for ways to predict major earthquakes. Today, research is carried out by seismologists throughout the world, especially in China, Japan, the Commonwealth of Independent States, and the United States. Knowing when earthquakes are likely to happen still baffles scientists everywhere. Minor tremors are sometimes followed by a big shock, but often they are not. The really big earthquake can happen without warning.

Seismic activity

Every day dozens of earthquakes are registered on seismographs in

A seismograph recording minor tremors on a seismogram as part of a constant worldwide watch on earthquakes.

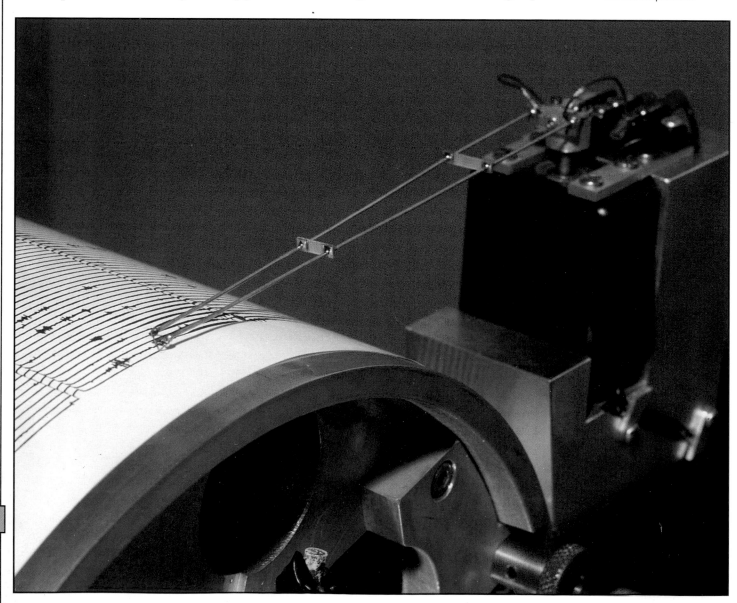

a worldwide network of stations. The seismograph is a sensitive instrument that can detect small shocks deep below the surface. By timing when the waves arrive, scientists can tell how far away the earthquake is and where its epicenter lies.

American scientists say that big earthquakes can be predicted if seismic activity increases over many years. They discovered that this happened in the years leading up to the San Francisco earthquakes of 1906, 1968, and 1989. But at other times seismographs were not able to predict earthquakes, such as the Tangshan earthquake of 1986.

Early recordings

The world's first instrument for measuring earthquakes was developed in China in the second century. A pendulum, hung in a bronze vessel, moved when an earthquake occurred. This caused one of the eight dragon mechanisms on the vessel to vibrate, so a ball fell out of its mouth and was caught by one of the toads underneath. This indicated the direction the seismic wave had come from.

The modern seismograph

Today's scientific recorders pick up the waves of energy from an earthquake and record the results on a seismogram.

The seismograph has a base that shakes with the earthquake. A pen is attached to a hanging weight, which remains still. The movements of the base cause the pen to record the vertical movements (1) and the horizontal movements (2) as graphs.

1

2

Surveying equipment

Some parts of the world are constantly monitored for earthquakes. The sophisticated equipment used records the changing levels of the land and the sea, and any changes in the movement or the makeup of rocks. The slightest movement in the earth's crust is detected by an American satellite known as LAGEOS. This stands for "Laser Geodynamic Satellite." It spins around the earth in orbit about 3,700 miles out. It has 426 prisms (or "eyes") on its dimpled surface, which note the tiniest shifts in the positions of the earth's plates. It will stay in orbit for many years.

Earthquakes are detected by using a variety of equipment.

Methods of Predicting Earthquakes

Natural indicators

Scientists still have a long way to go before they can predict earthquakes successfully, but some people have seen strange happenings that let them know an earthquake is about to occur. In the winter of 1988 people living in Quebec, Canada, saw a spectacular display of natural fireworks. Fireballs in the night sky spurted a luminous spray. Houses, trees, and clouds lit up with yellow-orange light, and colored rays appeared in the sky. Geologists checked the reports of these sightings with seismic records and found that the lights had appeared when a series of tremors had occurred.

In China it has been found that animals are able to sense vibrations in the earth before people. Snakes emerge from their holes in freezing weather, rats leave their buildings, while dogs and cats shiver and sometimes run about like ants.

1. Observatory with laser equipment
2. Surveys to show changes in land level
3. Measuring changes in the earth's magnetic field
4. Recording earthquakes on a seismograph
5. Measuring the speed at which rocks move past each other
6. Measuring changes in land level
7. Measuring the earth's gravity
8. Measuring strain on rocks

Below: Scientists in the 1970s preparing to launch the satellite LAGEOS, which records underground plate movements.

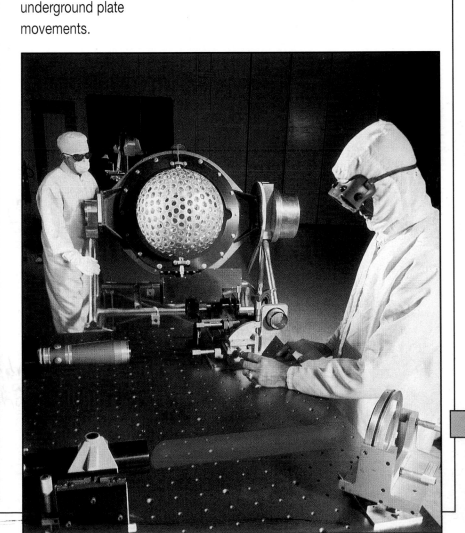

In recent years, many nations have joined in relief and rescue operations after major disasters have occurred. Governments have given large sums of money. Charities have sent out people carrying medical supplies, food, clothing, and bedding to devastated areas.

Special help

The International Rescue Corps (IRC) was formed in Britain in 1980 after an earthquake hit southern Italy, killing 3,000 people. The IRC carries medicine, relief supplies, radio

Left below: The sequence of events following an earthquake.

Start program of earthquake education

Assess overall damage caused

Begin rebuilding using earthquake-resistant materials

Immediate rescue of people

Restore communications and economic activity

Assess human needs (food, water, shelter)

Assess condition of buildings

Distribute emergency aid

The Red Cross is the official rescue team here at the scene of an earthquake. They carry basic life-saving equipment with them.

equipment, and machines that can detect people trapped in disaster-hit regions. The volunteers are on standby 24 hours a day and work closely with governments, the UN, the International Red Cross, and relief organizations.

Cleaning up

Specialist teams from the United Nations, the United States, Canada, and Europe have also taken part in clearing away the wreckage, restoring water, gas, and electricity, and telling people how they can rebuild their homes. Survivors of an earthquake often do not want to move away from the earthquake region that has always been their home. Many towns flattened by earthquakes have risen again and again on the same spot.

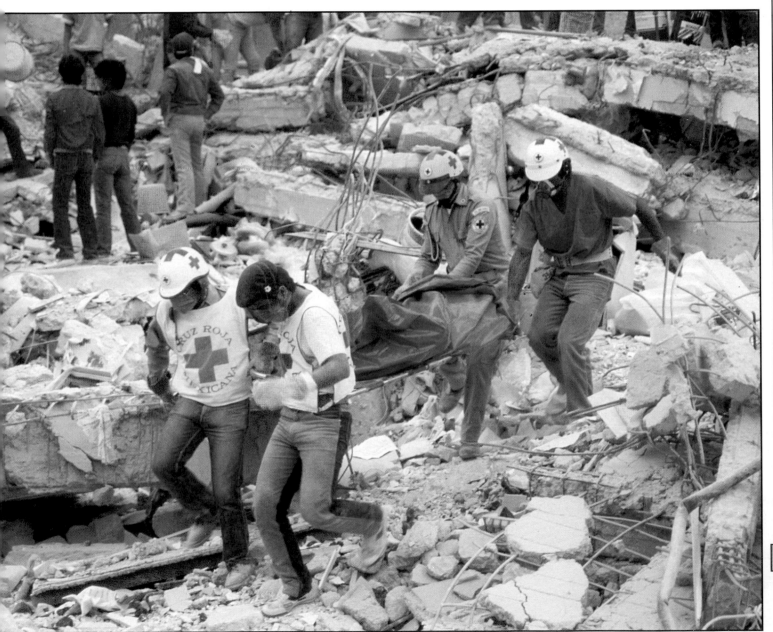

One way to reduce the loss of life caused by earthquakes is to predict when they will occur and then move everybody who is at risk out of the area. Another way is to make sure that buildings they live in are sited, designed, and built so as to resist an earthquake's tremors.

Today scientists are able to pinpoint the areas that are most likely to be hit by earthquakes.

This wood framed building fell down because it was not firmly fixed to its foundations.

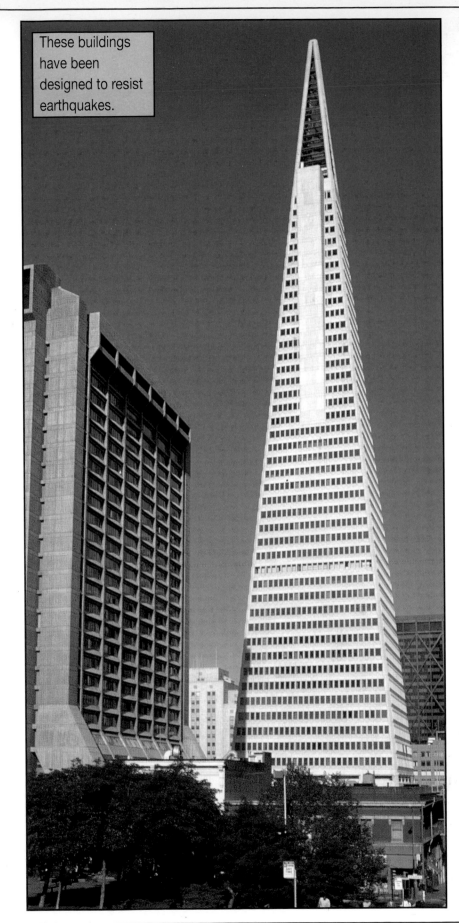

These buildings have been designed to resist earthquakes.

Most of these areas lie along fault lines, and in places where the ground can be rocked by vibrations. When a big earthquake occurs, planners could think about rebuilding the town in a new and safer location. But more often they will try to find ways of rebuilding it in the same place and making it as earthquake-proof as possible.

Building design

Buildings can be designed so that the impact of the earthquake is lessened. For instance, it has been found that buildings made of wood are less likely to fall down than ones made of brick, but they must stand on solid ground. A light roof does not cause as much damage when it falls as one made of heavy tiles. All buildings need to stand on solid rock or have firm foundations.

Buildings need to "give" when the earth vibrates, so they must be flexible. Skyscrapers built with steel frames will sway from side to side without falling because of their flexibility.

Preventing destruction

It is not possible to make some areas of the world totally earthquake-proof, but it is hoped the damage can be lessened as much as possible to prevent major disasters from occurring in the future.

1. Project Challenge

Survivors of earthquakes urgently need shelter, and tents are often not suitable for extremes of climate. Can you design a better unit to be made using low-cost materials?

Remember that emergency supplies are usually air-freighted to disaster sites, but since large planes cannot always land, the cargoes are lowered to the ground as the plane flies slowly. Space is vital, so your unit must pack flat and be simple to assemble with no special tools.

Materials:
Shoe boxes or cardboard
Adhesive tape and fasteners
Note pad and pencil
Scissors

Method:

1. List your basic needs for survival. Discuss these with others.

2. Sketch some ideas for a shelter. Draw a plan of what you think your model will look like.

3. Build your model from stiff cardboard very carefully to scale.

4. Decide what should go inside your shelter.

Plan

ENDS 6 × 6

SIDES 10 × 6

TOP/BOTTOM 10 × 6

Portable Toilet

Water out

Water in

Ventilation

Power supply

Shelter

Insulation

Flooring

Water in

Water out

2. Lightweight houses for earthquake zones

In regions where earthquakes are common, buildings are made of lightweight materials that allow the whole structure to be flexible. In Japan, wood is used for framework and then covered with thin boarding or tensioned paper screen. This allows for ground movement, and is less dangerous if violent tremors cause the building to collapse.

Method:

1. Decide on the type of house that you would like to build.

2. Make the walls of your house. Cut the straws to length and attach to a pin board. Glue cardboard triangles to the corners and let it dry.

3. When the wall frames are dry, cover them with tissue paper and glue in place. When the glue is dry, spray the tissue with water to tension it. Assemble the walls with strips of adhesive tape.

4. Cut a piece of cardboard to the roof size. Score and fold for the ridge. Stick strips of straws onto the roof and when dry, attach to the walls with adhesive tape.

Materials:
Art straws
Waterproof glue
Thin cardboard
Tissue paper
Adhesive tape
Pin board and pins
Plant mist spray with clean water

Walls

Glue

Pin board

Straws

Tissue paper

Straws

Cardboard

Roof

Finished house

GLOSSARY

CRUST The layer of rock at the earth's surface.

EPICENTER The position on the earth's surface above the focus of an earthquake.

FAULT A large crack or break in a series of rocks. This is where two parts of the earth can slip past each other.

GEOLOGIST A scientist who studies the origin, history, structure, and processes of the earth.

INFERNO A huge, roaring fire.

LANDSLIDE A mass of loose rock and soil that slides down a steep slope.

LUMINOUS Radiating light.

MAGNITUDE The size of an earthquake as measured on the Richter scale.

MERCALLI SCALE A measure of an earthquake's intensity, ranging from 1 to 12.

PLATES Giant slabs of underground rocks, often bigger than continents.

RED CROSS The international organization formed to care for the sick, wounded, and homeless in wartime and also during natural disasters.

RELIEF SUPPLIES Cargoes of food, water, medicines, clothing, tents, and huts sent to disaster areas.

RICHTER SCALE A scale ranging from 1 to 10 used to show the size of an earthquake.

SATELLITE A human-made object circling the earth.

SEISMOGRAPH A sensitive instrument used to detect force and position of earth tremors.

SHOCK WAVES The waves of energy that are produced underground as rocks snap. When they reach the surface they cause violent shaking.

STRESS The intensity of two forces working against each other.

TREMORS The shaking caused by earthquakes.

TSUNAMI A large sea wave, sometimes called a tidal wave, caused by an earthquake.

VIBRATION A continuous shaking movement.

BOOKS TO READ

Earthquake!
by Jules Archer (Macmillan Child Group, 1991)

How Did We Find Out about Earthquakes?
by Isaac Asimov (Walker & Co., 1978)

Earthquake
by Brian Knapp (Steck-Vaughn, 1990)

Volcanoes & Earthquakes
by Mary Elting (Simon & Schuster, 1990)

Earthquake
by Christopher Lampton (Millbrook Press, 1991)

Earthquakes
by Ed Radlauer and Ruth Radlauer (Children's Press, 1987)

Predicting Earthquakes
by Gregory Vogt (Franklin Watts, 1989)

Picture acknowledgments

The publishers would like to thank the following for allowing their photographs to be reproduced in this book: Associated Press/Topham *cover*, 19 (right); Colorific! 14 (Alon Reininger/Contact), 24/25 (Frank Fournier/Contact); Frank Lane Picture Agency 10; Photri 12, 13, 23, 27; Picturepoint Ltd 4/5 (both); Science Photo Library 2/3 (Peter Menzel), 9 (David Parker), 20 (Tom McHugh), 26 bottom (Peter Menzel); Frank Spooner Pictures Ltd 16/17, 18/19.

INDEX